Words *Can Explain*

Sha Rene'

A Collection of Poems

authorHOUSE®

AuthorHouse™
1663 Liberty Drive, Suite 200
Bloomington, IN 47403
www.authorhouse.com
Phone: 1-800-839-8640

© 2007 Sharon Rene Summers. All rights reserved.

No part of this book may be reproduced, stored in a retrieval system, or transmitted by any means without the written permission of the author.

First published by AuthorHouse 12/10/2007

ISBN: 978-1-4343-5441-9 (e)
ISBN: 978-1-4343-4761-9 (sc)
ISBN: 978-1-4343-4762-6 (hc)

Library of Congress Control Number: 2007909863

Printed in the United States of America
Bloomington, Indiana

This book is printed on acid-free paper.

Book cover design concept by: Summer's Day

Summer's Day Publishing
10 Schalks Crossing Road 501-147
Plainsboro, New Jersey 08016

*F*irst I was born and there was pain
*O*h for I let out in the rain
*R*unning and jumping through puddles
*E*ver does the
*V*iolet shine
*E*ver is the
Rainbow

Digital Photography by:
James J. Kriegsmann Jr. Manhattan, NY

Words Can Explain

"The Mozart Song"

"I like Mozart and theatre and wine
I like quiet places to dine
I like water although I don't swim
Don't like staying at movies till the end
I like fast cars, chiffon scarves, large-brim hats
and electric guitars
and you think you know me"

An excerpt from the poem turned into lyrics written
by Sha Rene'
entitled
"A Mozart Song"

Sha René
A Collection of Poems
Sha Rene' has written over 250 songs and over 200 poems.

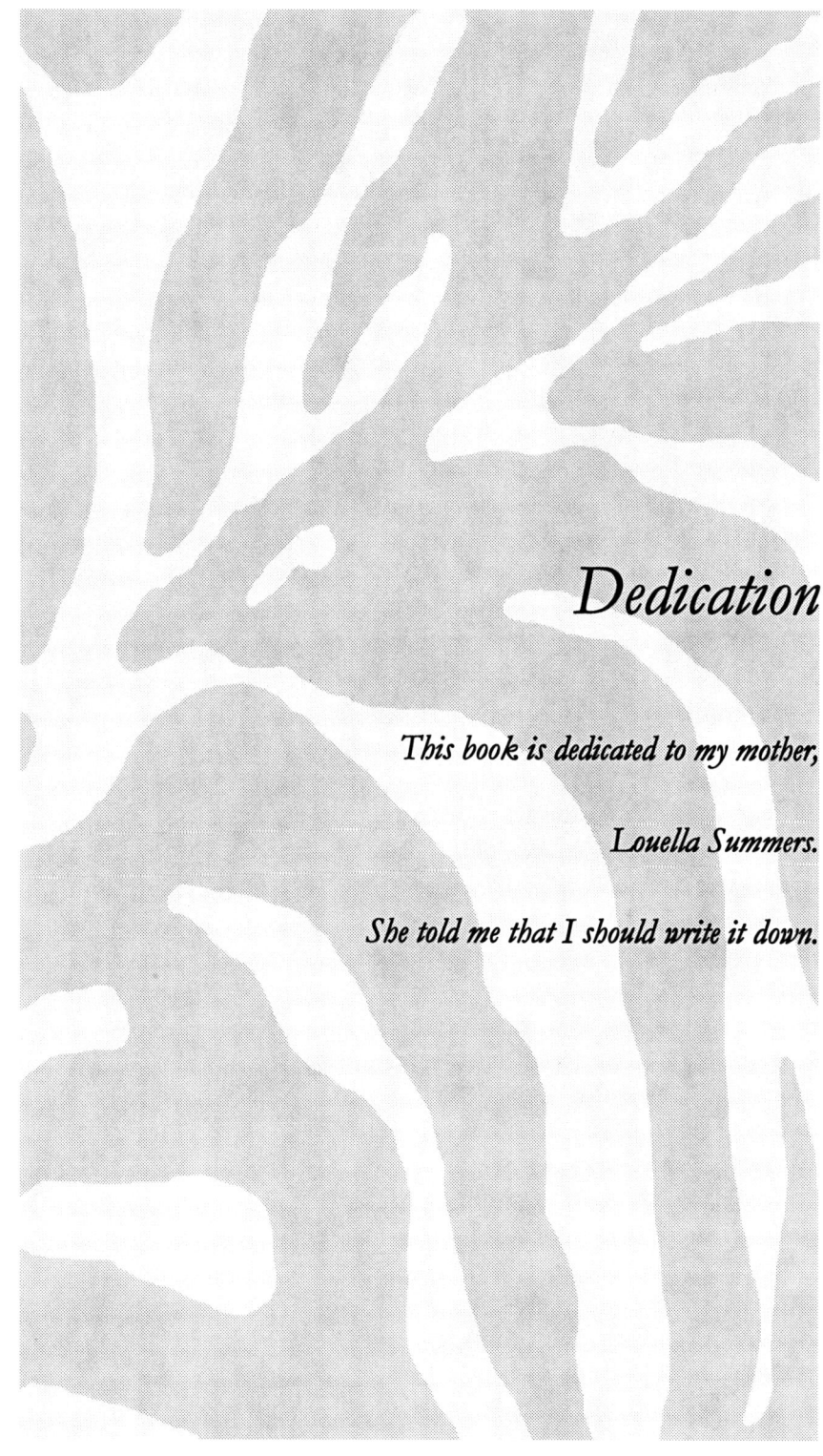

Dedication

This book is dedicated to my mother,

Louella Summers.

She told me that I should write it down.

Contents

Dedication	ix
Preface	xiii
"Namesake"	1
Circus Ole'	3
"I'm Falling"	5
"Naked"	7
"Black Man"	9
"A Walk"	11
"Don't Bother Me"	13
"And the Phone Rings"	15
"Color"	17
"Carrying"	19
"I wanted to"	21
"Mine"	23
"A Home"	25
"Life"	27
"Stages"	28
"Cartwheel"	31
"I'm Sorry Langston"	33
"Open"	35
"Dealin'"	37
"Did I"	39
"The Tarot"	41
"A Lie"	43
"Corporate Blue"	45
"Mixed Up"	47
"Roots"	49
"Orgasm"	51
"Standing for a Moment"	53
"Trust me I did"	55
"Your Voice"	57
"The Lottery"	59
"Me Jane"	61
"An American Dream"	63
"Bigger"	65

"Live This"	67
"Sesame Street"	69
"A place in my heart"	71
"Sight"	73
"Extensions"	77
"Show me the way"	80
"I Promise"	83
"Substance"	85
"Mi-Self"	87
"Shame"	89
"Monday thru Sunday Girl"	91
"Garden of Evil"	93
"Know That I Loved You"	97
"A Rain Dance"	101
"First Person"	105
"Escapade"	109
"Wrong"	113
"Blank as a Linen-Colored Rule"	115
"Anyplace, Anywhere, Anytime"	117
"The lady in the wheelchair"	119
"I still do"	121
"Master"	123
"This is not a Poetry Slam"	125
"And over there to the right on the bass"	129
"Ain't That Good News"	131
"Dis-Closure"	133
"To the Black Poet"	141
Djembre	143
"Great Love"	145
"A Crossroads"	147
"A Black Woman's Song"	149
"Am I?"	155
"The Ball"	157
"Daylight"	160
"White Butterfly"	163
Write	167
Oscar Night	169

Preface

I can remember as a child having a lot to say, and I decided to write it down. I wanted to express myself in a way that few could really understand, and it didn't matter that I used words like a pencil or a brush of color sweeping across the pages. Since then, I have wanted to speak out loud, so here I am presenting this gift to you.

This will be my first published book of my poetry, Words Can Explain. Later, I will release my early works to you, Thoughts Come to Mind, as seen through the eyes of myself at 10 years old. These books are what I have dreamed of for a very long time, and now they have become real to me.

For many years as a singer/songwriter I wrote lyrics. I also wrote words that I felt did not need music, and here they are. Sing with me. Sing with me.

The Author

"Namesake"

This is for my mother
This is for my mother who picked cotton
And hurt her hands as a child
I would always wonder if it's harder now
And know that if it were me I would only be a problem
I am not the quiet type
And nor was she
And she taught me to fight for everything I believe
in
cluding
This
This piece of work
That I share with you
For all the pain
For her
Namesake
I wish you peace
Although my words may hurt
Although my words are strong
I find truth in knowing
I can tell
what's right
and
what's wrong

Circus Ole'

They hang you every day out to dry
and then you have no energy left
not even to sigh
all you wish to do is get out
go away
have the freedom
that was given to you
when the day is risen to the sun
and you have yet to begin your journey
Don't tell me that you made a mistake
by hating me
I have had no reason to give you an answer
when the questions you ask
go around in circles
and fly when balloons
have no air
Round the issues
round the problems
round about
Let's get together
it's not hard to figure it out
that the 60-foot woman
can tear you apart
and it's her smarts that scare you
Circus
it's just a circus that you pay a pretty penny for
Ole'
Ole'

"I'm Falling"

*And I can barely move my feet now
because I have no reason
to dance
And I can hardly try to
sing now
See I don't have a second chance
I'm falling
in so deep
I can hardly sleep
I'm falling
into the sky
I don't know why I still love you
And I can barely hold my
head up
because I've done something to you
And I can hardly stand up
See I have to believe in you
I'm falling
from such a high
I can hardly fly now
into the blue
Can't get over
you
you
you*

"Naked"

I am naked
and I am writing these words to you
I am naked
and I am thinking of what it's worth to you
I am naked
and at your doorstep is a pillow
Watch me dressing
though I don't want to fall
I am naked
Do you hear me whisper a trilogy
I am naked
and bound to disbeliefs
Who are you
if you don't know me
I am naked
and it's too late now
to take a picture
I am crawling
on a river
that does not exist
Sing to me now
'cause I am listening
not to a sound
I am naked
and I can't tell you how it feels
You have to try it for yourself

"Black Man"

If I don't explain to you
Black man
If I don't speak to you
Black man
If I don't guide you
Black man
will you grow?
If I don't bear you
Black man
If I don't include you
Black man
If I don't respect you
Black man
will you know?
If I don't shame you
Black man
and I don't blame you
Black man
Can you see me?
If I don't encourage you
Black man
I will discourage you
Black man
and you will never be
the Black man
you should be

"A Walk"

*I took a long walk today
and passed churches and the parks
and saw people
doing the things they normally do
and I wanted to be part of it all
of the wheelchair
pushing
and seeing
and walking
and the running for the bus
and jumping rope
I took a long walk today
and saw black and white streets
and paper bags
and airplanes and I stop
just to capture
a glimpse of time*

"Don't Bother Me"

Am I angry?
Oh hell yeah!
When the only thing
you have to say to me
is the only thing
you don't want no one else to hear
Don't bother me

"And the Phone Rings"

And you came along
to make me smile
for a while
has come and gone
and I am still laughing
no longer crying
for times long gone
And you came along
quiet as a whisper
I am here since her
and you don't have to look
anymore
Yes you came along
and now I see longer
larger than my eyes
have ever known
And now the phone rings

"Color"

If you cloud your mind with Color
then you will only see
in
Black or White

"Carrying"

Today I changed my hair
back to my nappy-headed self with dark-colored curls
Today I changed my attitude
I have the need to be close to my afrocentric self
Today I took off my shoes and wore sandals
took off my under-wire
How I felt like the queen adored
with my naked breasts
and only a skirt
and my jewels
and my shoulders no longer worn
from carrying

"I wanted to"

I wanted to tell you
how you should feel
although I don't know you
I wanted to explain

that I could give these things to you
without hurting you
in any way

I wanted to take you away in my mind
to a place you've been before in a dream
that you cannot remember
and I've dreamed it also many times

The fantasy was a present to you from me
and I lay awake at night
thinking of how to make it better

Better is the thought
I'd bring to you just to make you smile again
not as a friend but as a partner
a partner in sharing the victory over imagination

I wanted you to know
that you could go away in your mind and be relaxed
and comfort with all that you feel
and it doesn't mean you have to touch

I wanted only to
make your body catch up with your mind
for a moment
only for a moment

I wanted to let you know
that anyone at any time could love you
because you make things easy

I wanted you to know
how lucky you are to have all the things you do
and enjoy them
Family is most near and dear to you

I wanted to share my thoughts
of you
with you

For this is what I wanted
I only wanted to

"Mine"

I can't change the way people view me
I can only project that which is in me
and sometimes
I don't even want to share this with you

"A Home"

There's a Tropical Island
in the middle of the desert
There's a Baseball field
in the middle of the sea
There's a place
I can't remember
that was there only for you and me
There's a child
in the middle of the ocean
There's a man in the middle of your mind
He is telling me things
I should not hear
but it's the place I will not find
It's a tear that never should have been
It's a tree
that will never come to grow
There's a house in the middle of the river
and a home
I will never come to know

"Life"

If life is a beach
why can't I find the water
If life is a train
why can't I get off here
if life is a sky
why are there so many clouds
covering the blue
If life is love
why can't I be with you

If life is rain
what is this umbrella
If life is snow
tell me why I'm melting
If life is a dream
why can't I wake up now
If life is love
why don't you know how

If life is the mall
why don't I have money
to buy anything I want
If life is a restaurant
why don't I ever get
just what I ordered
If life is a mountain
how can I climb without shoes
If life is love how did I lose you

"Stages"

Read a book
without flipping the pages
Drive a car
without turning the key
Find a telephone number
you haven't dialed for ages
Take the time to talk with me
Drink a drink
without lifting the glass
and no you didn't have a straw
Cry a tear
without feeling the pain
till you can't cry anymore
Give a gift
that was meant for someone else
losing all its meaning
Dream a dream
you had before
and almost lost its meaning
Tie a knot
so loose that it falls apart
simply by pulling
shoot the gun for the heck of it
not knowing who you're killing
Take time for granted
each and every day
thinking it will just stop for you

*Doing things you don't want to
just because you have to do
I can't possibly
make you believe that
I can read a book
without flipping the pages
Just remember
all things go through
Stages*

"Cartwheel"

Let me tell you a tale
about the water
Let me whisper in your eyes
Let me show you a reason
for gladness
without the usual disguise

Let me tell you I'll climb any mountain
or travel across the sea
Let me ride on a Cartwheel forever
if you are to be with me
Show me the reasons

Why does the glass
seem to always break
Show me the lessons learned
Don't make me a promise
you will only break

"I'm Sorry Langston"

I always thought
poetry was for space cadets
for intellect
for people who had no heads
but I was wrong

I'll never forget
"Hold fast to Dreams"

for if dreams die
and why?

"Open"

Is it that I feel
so complete with you
Is it just my mind
making up things
I want to
Is it that I give my soul
or spread my wings
to find a place

Is it you
that brings your heart to me
Is it that for you
I set you free
or did your mind
just find home
for a moment

I sometimes wonder
why you don't talk to me
during the time
when I most need
but how are you to know
that I want to show you everything
I have to give
and more

You touch me
By just staring into my eyes
The me you see

is only a disguise
because no one
can see me but you

You thrill me
with every waking heartbeat
It is still me
who opens the door to love

"Dealin'"

He hits you
and you're dealin'
He curses you
and you're dealin'
He cheats on you
now you're dealin'
He makes you wait
and you're dealin'
he takes things away
and you're dealin'
he breaks what you make
and you're dealin'
He throws out the food
and you're dealin'
He ruins your mood
so you're dealin'
He lies to your face
and you're dealin'
runs over your place
and you're dealin'
Doesn't open the door
and you're dealin'
He throws you to the floor
and you're dealin'
This will poem will end
when you are tired of dealin'

"Did I"

Did I ask for these things
that have been given to me
Did I ask for an explanation
Did I wave my hand across the sky and cry
Did I ask for these things that are not known to me
Did I ask for a reason
or opportunity
Did I dance across a cloud
and look down and see the you in me
and are you here
Did I scream at the top of my lungs
when I know I had no breath
Did I ask you although you were there
Please forgive me for not understanding
Did I ask for these things that bring people joy
to a girl or a boy
who sit and won't take their eyes away
from me
Did I ask for the kindness you have shown me today
for others
Did I forsake you only because I did not understand your power
Your meaning to be the only forever
in my life

"The Tarot"

And I spoke to the Tarot
It told me things
already known to me
Yes
I have seen my souls
dance around tables
and kick over footstools
and climb to rooftops
to do unscrupulous things
and look at steeples
and touch red tapestry walls
Yes, I have talked to the Tarot
and found my mate
and I have always known
him today
yesterday
before

"A Lie"

I have many things
Clothes, purses, handbags, shoes, gloves, hats, toys, lamps, plants, couches, paintings, ties
What a lie
I have told myself

"Corporate Blue"

Strength is not letting it get to you
When you walk in the door
In your corporate blue
and "You're Fired"
But when you said it had to be that
In the office
I pull my hair back
Never stare
And shine a smile
That you can see anywhere or
Down the corridor for miles
And they play more games than I played as a child
They play hockey
When they beat each other over the head with a stick
Guess what?
John has locked his door
And did you see that secretary go in for more
And he says "It wasn't me"
She buttoned her blouse came out
And got a raise
She has the office and is very rude
I am in "Corporate Blue" and I'm in the cube
I go in the bathroom stall and take open my braids
Is that all yours?
I hear the white girls say
I get up at 6:30 am
I'm 5 minutes late and I drive in the rain
Oh no the clock is not fixed and has not been fixed since the boss had his trick

I get my performance review
It's just a written script
But I have no idea who is in this play
I gotta pay my bills
Damn I feel ill
Well I guess its Cap'n Crunch for lunch for me today
I can't wait to burn every suit
I keep lookin' at my college degree
Every time they fire me

"Mixed Up"

It is too funny when somebody calls you
The N-word
And somebody calls you
"White girl" all on the same day
What a world

"Roots"

I would swing from a chandelier if I had one
I would sit right under a tree
and look above to see which leaf is falling
right in front of me by my feet
and stand, lift my head, and take in a breeze you see
because and only because one day I will be under a tree
and the leaf will fall
So now I can smell the fresh green
and capture in my mind what a scene
and all I can think now is that I want to share it
take a picture and show it and dare you to tear it
I must have someone to show it to
Could it be you?
So I dance with my feet in the wind
I am over my head
and as I balance myself
I do an upside-down tango
You see I see better with my hands on the ground
like a root I hear a sound calling
I cannot find my roots standing because it is as if I have never fallen
and fall I must in order to stand tall
Yes, I would swing from a chandelier if I had one
It is the sun with its rays and its crystal raindrops
that fall
my body is heavy
I will only land on my feet that I really don't know at all
You see I see better with my hands on the ground
Please won't someone turn me upside down?

"Orgasm"

Tremble you make me
with desire
And you make me burn
How I burn
Shaking I am continuously
as you please me
And as I fall to my knees
now I can sleep

"Standing for a Moment"

*It was years ago where
I sat in the same place
and how much younger
was I then
It was years ago
I walked the street
glancing at time
Is time my friend
I close my eyes and I can see me running
in a yellow dress from a bumble bee
I'm still running
and I have yet to be stung
One day I just may stand for a moment
just to see
what it feels like*

"Trust me I did"

Everybody tells me
I don't listen
My Dad said that when I was 8
My teacher, my Mom, my Brother
Then when I got older
my boyfriend and my boss
So how come
I know just what everybody said
I know my Dad complained about money
and my Teacher yelled at the kids in the back of the room
and my Mom yelled about the neighbors parked across her driveway
and my brother told me I should get a cheaper apartment
and my boyfriend told me he was too busy to call
and my boss told me I wasn't good enough
You see I heard just what you said
It's just that you just didn't like
that I talked over you
or maybe rolled my eyes
or asked you why
or coughed in between your words that were mean
You see I heard every word you said
Its just that I only want to hear the positive
I push away the negative
So I'm sorry you thought I didn't hear you
Trust me I did

"Your Voice"

I can hear in your voice
Words that call out to me
Words that will set me free
I can hear in your voice
time that won't slip away
Time you have given me today
to get to know you
Love I can feel it so
though I want you near me
I can hear in your voice
truth that you know is real
Truth and you know the deal
And if you play your cards right
you may win
I can hear in your voice
pleasure that you will give
pleasure that is to live
with the one who can love you
Seek if you will the wine
The splendor of not
when the magic that I feel
I can hear in your voice
Me
'cause I feel the same
Me
and I know my name
has a sound

"The Lottery"

People take chances
Chances on a dream
that some strange set of numbers
will give them what they need
At 8:00 they sit glaring
Glaring

"Me Jane"

I woman
Woman that I am
Am meant
Am built
With no guilt
And I am your friend
I woman
To the one who sees the other woman
Makes idols
And pictures
Of things
That I can't be
Makes cherries
And incense
And trinkets
To adore
Makes life even sometimes
On the carpet or the floor
I woman
Have to captivate
Should never be raped
I woman
Breathe of life
Life of death
Death for a new beginning
Hears voices and things I am feeling
or dreaming

So listen to I
Woman
The bearer
The bearer of all burdens
And I still love
I woman

"An American Dream"
In memory of the WTC and all its people of 9/11

Where were you when it happened
that 2 jets trashed the sky
and lives were taken
and we were shaken from the tallest buildings so high
A bright light
I never thought could stand
America
tall and proud
to be an American it never seemed
I would want to scream aloud
White, Black, Jew, Muslim, Hindu
It doesn't matter at all
Every nation today has to stand tall
for the American dream let freedom reign
And maybe Martin's wish
will now not be in vain
to be an American never meant this
Never meant, kill maim
Live as though you don't believe
God knows your name
As long as you haven't forgotten
what life really means
I now have an "American Dream"

"Bigger"
My Native Son

I've tried so many times to exist
yet you don't let me
Don't let me breathe
let me be me
and it's right now I think of Bigger
and everyone who cares
should know who he is
I understand the collar
so tight and metal and pain
and although I have not worn it
it's passed through my veins
passed through only because I noticed it
only because I took the time to look
at causes and effects
only because I hear the chains
and the hooks that still rattle on his neck
How they don't stop until I ignore
Why should I have to?
Why should I have to?
Why make believe it was never there?
How I've tried so many times to exist
You don't let me breathe
It's right now that I think of Bigger
You are everywhere I go
My Native Son

"Live This"

Together we can conquer the world
Do great things
Make plans that will last
Above all things
Together we can watch the sun
It seems
we were
together
We can dance under the moon
and what do we do when this world is doomed
Do we continue to dance?
or drink up a storm
while we look at December days
that are too damn warm
What do we do
in the dream of despair
when all we needed was Love to get us to somewhere
What does it take to hang on
when the chance of surviving
in a dust cloud
Though the streets are too long
Why just can't we be together
What is wrong with this?
I guess I don't have a choice but to picture this
Imagine this
Live this
alone

"Sesame Street"

The faces are small
the grins fight to show
although we know it's there
somewhere
Don't listen to the words they say
because they only repeat what they hear
hear on TV
hear in the street
hear at home while at the makeshift dinner table
hear on the playground
from another the same size as he
Close your eye instead of open
maybe you won't be damaged
damaged by all around you
because you don't have
your own private Sesame Street
Cry child
Cry
because you don't even know
what the grass is for

"A place in my heart"

I find a place in my heart for the one
who heals me
for the one who has come into
my private space and made me reach out
for the one who doesn't find it hard
to show me how he feels

I find a place in my mind for the one
who has pleasant thoughts
of things
that will make me smile
places we could go together
in this world of ours

I find a place in my soul for the one
who makes me believe
that I am real
that I am here to spread my wings
before him

I find a place in my body for the one
who will help me grow
and share all I want to share
and give my body the one touch
I wish to know

I find a place in my heart
for you

"Sight"

Trials
Tribulations
Drama
Problems
Stress
Issues
Boredom
Solve them
Situations
People
Grieving
For this nation
To stand up
and rise up
To be
Hate
Fate
Degradation
No where
No how
Disbelief
Apparent
Suicide
In this world
Where
Life has no meaning
No reason
To be

Prostitution
Illusions
Past
Present
Disease
Please help me
All I want is to be
Time
The mind
Trouble
Waters
Screaming
Leaning
Yearning
To exist to me
Grass
Greener
Streets
Cleaner
Love
Treat him
To be
Kind
Sweeter
Patient
Not Weaker
Soul Seeker
Teach her
To dream

Truth
Child bearer
Dare her
To think
World
Maker
Please
Help
Us
to see

"Extensions"

Since I was part White and part Black
I never knew what to do with my hair
I'd comb and rake
a very large afro and why did I dare go to church
in Shirley Temple curls
Straightening out and ironing
and perms were not for me
I never knew what to do with my hair

Too straight for curls
Too kinky for ponies
too long for pageboys
too short for flips

I'd tease and tease
and find myself damaging
taking away the softness
I'd hire a hairdresser
and somehow he'd find
everything about my hair
that makes it all worth it

The bounce
the shine
the length
the gloss
the color
the toss

I'd be beautiful for a night
at the 50-dollar cost

I couldn't do that every day

So I looked beyond
the natural way
and found alternative beauty
You have no reason
to get mad at me
Why
because I long not to be white
but to feel free and have the waves
hit the middle of my back
have the wind blow my curls
or have the hair hit my face
so I don't know where I'm at
Hiding like a girl
a strand within my mouth
I have to pull away
an the compliments
I seem to get now everyday

A man's touch at the ends of my hair
with his fingers through
creating
a sensation
I'd love to know again
and again

or

*the strong pull or tug
that he gets from my hair
when holding my head in his hands
beckoning for his pleasure*

*What's wrong in finding
the alternative beauty?*

*I go to the shop
where I may choose
from long, short, straight, curly, blonde or brunette
and you thought I bought a wig I bet*

I did not but found the pieces of splendor

*Some call it extensions
Some call it weave
but it's my alternative beauty
I've found I believe that makes me smile
inside
and I grow*

"Show me the way"

Show me the way
do not lead me down the path
of make believe
i've been there before
Show me the way
don't lead me to a river
that never ends
i can't swim
Show me the way
don't tell me you've seen colors
when only there
was grey
and i can't forget
no i won't forget
how u showed me the
way
and i learned something
yes i learned something
something that u didn't think
u were tellin' me
i closed my eyes and made believe
i couldn't see
i went down a path
and found a river
and i'd swim to the end
and saw that grey could be a color
and i forgot

how i must forget
or i will
drive me
crazy
is this the end
why am i askin' you?

"I Promise"

*I can in no way determine
that which is going to be
tomorrow
For it alone is not promised
Even a promise
that you make to yourself
including no one else
has a great possibility
of not being kept
a promise
to do something
tomorrow
maybe the keyword
is
tomorrow*

"Substance"

Somehow I know you know me
although it's not real
Somehow you feel me
with your soul
I have a picture in my mind
You are not very young
or very old
Through disbelief in things
that can be
I have known you
close before
I want to see you
though not distant
Time aside
Let's put time aside
to see the things that can be
I need you to know
I've never done
things wild or crazy
I need you to think

"Mi-Self"

I wonder if you will be pleased
with my imperfections
as I see them
but somehow
they are always appreciated

I walk down a main street
not looking at anyone but
mi-self
through the glass window
where my reflection is cast
before me

I primp
I smile
and I fix my hair
or redo a lip
stick
and stare
Is this obvious?

I love me
and I can't help it
and somehow people
have always found something wrong
in that

I look in the mirror
and I am pleased
at what i see
including the roundness
and the little extra fat
that i carry along with me
and the rest of the world

For some reason
I am still pleased

'cause I am of mi-self
this shows
is that why
you can't stay away from me?

"Shame"

Sometimes
when it's cloudy outside
you can see the sun
Sometimes
when it's sunny inside
you can hear the rain
Last night
I heard a baby cry
and cry
and cry
what a shame

"Monday thru Sunday Girl"

Don't wanna be your Monday girrl
your Tuesday girrl
your Wednesday girrl
Don't wanna be your Thursday girrl
your Friday girrl
your Saturday girrl
I wanna be your
Monday thru Sunday girl
Give that a whirl!

"Garden of Evil"

Garden of Evil son of man
Sing to the mountain tops
Oh take my hand
Praise to the ages
Of kings that could be
If you could make me
Your Black woman
The queen I should be
Sing of a needle
Not from a sewing stitch
Make sure it's the right time
To call me your cliché
Talk to your sons
To make them a man
Don't lose Respect
For the Black Woman I am
Tie your Bow tie
Your shoe lace
Your cross
Make sure they tell you
That you are the boss
Don't lose it chile
It's worth more than you
For God is now angry
With the drugs that you do
Don't blame me your Sista'
for preaching the cause
'Cause I am Black woman

Without me
You're lost
Garden of Evil
Please don't take my away my king
'Cause I am here standing
Expecting a ring
I see my White sistas
Dancing a dream
And I am Black woman
That's all that it seems
Don't give my brother
Toys, gifts, clothes
Shoes for his feet
Let him work, slave
Deserve to have his family eat
Don't blame my father
For walking away
Black man wake up
Today's a new day
Garden of Evil
Makes my man feel weak
So he hustles
And kills
And lives in the street
Where is my model
My upward mobility
My Lover, my friend
My peace, tranquility?

Yes I am Black woman
Working hard from day to day
That is no reason
For you to walk away
Don't be afraid that I might pass you
'Cause I got A's and B's
It's only your fault
That you only got C's
But I do not blame you
Not you alone
'Cause you did not get this way
All on your own
With the help
of the Garden of Evil
Yet in the midst of your reach
Yes, I am Black woman
and I am here to teach you
Black man
To stay out of
The Garden
For there is no fruit
For you to bear
Please don't resent me
'Cause I get somewhere

"Know That I Loved You"

This is the last thing I will say to you on this night
I have thought this over and dread having to say what is on my mind
Knowing that I have loved you a thousand times
This is the last thing that I shall say to you
As I think about the smiles we shared and the laughter and the touch now I seem
not to bear to think of
in a dream
This is the last thing I have to say to you 'cause
With you I really cared
I dare now not to think of things that might have been
Were we ever friends?
This is the last thing I can say to you because I am choking on my own words and
it's nice that you notice
how I am with words but these words today are for you
This is the last thing I will say to you
'Cause I am hurt and I can't hurt no more
I can think of the kisses and the hugs that were missing and then all of a sudden
you started kissing and
I lost my head
But I forgive me
This is the last thing I want to say to you like
My body with yours and we aren't really touching even though there is nothing
between us
And inner
Secrets
Sheets
River flowing me not knowing the whole time
Where your heart was

97

Where your mind was
When I was in your place of content
Is that what you meant?
That I was just a thing
And not good enough for a ring?
This is the last thing I say to you 'cause
I am torn up and worn out and tossed out and rung out like a towel you just used
to wipe down your car
on a rainy damn day!
I know where I am going
I am going to a place where I can share my grief with a million and one…that
one is me
A million and one sistas who understand my pain
Let's just talk about it
And….
If you are still awake after I kick you out of my bed you were never in
Then wake up my brother
It's me and only me who could ever be your friend and I…
This is the last thing I wish to say to you 'cause
Wishing for a star to fly above my head so I can wish you with me was the
stupidest thing I could ever
dreamt of doing
And yet I stand here still
And the sky is black
Dark
Not a cloud in the sky
This is the last thing I might say to you if you are ever standing in front of me
with her or him or
whomever you devoted your time to and don't tell me it was the job
I cry

And I can't sleep
And I don't eat
And I can't see
But I tell you this now
Know that I loved you
Right now my stomach hurts and I can't speak words and words are something I know well
Words are the only thing I have and I can use them and they will l let me use them
For whatever purpose I see
So right now know that every word I say I really mean
Goodbye!

"A Rain Dance"

Dancing around time
Time that I do not understand
Time that lends itself to its own being
Time that wraps itself around my hand
Time that looks at me from the wall
Time that calls out to me each and every morning with a loud beeping sound
Or a song
Dancing, Dancing around time
'Cause this dance has to end
The prom night
The wedding dance
The monster's ball
A spiritual dance in the sand
Dancing around time
Wasting all it gives to you
Is a shame and I can't blame anyone but you
Because I spent my time
Worrying
Crying
Sad
Over you
Dancing around time
When you may not see it every day
It reminds us all that this too shall pass away
Dancing around time
'Cause you are dancing around your dreams
It seems
Is a mystery to me

Dance
Sing
Shout
Scream
Live
Love
Dream
But do
Make things happen
Make things happen for you
Dancing around time
Makes me think of my mom that's passed
And I think of all the things she meant that will last
Dancing and Dancing and singing a song
Was what she wanted to do after that long day
Of pickin' cotton in an Indian headdress
And her dreams
Yes her dreams of becoming a free person
That seemed so long
Where her hands didn't have to hurt
And people could stop cursin'
And Dancing around her time
But a short dance and a dream
Brought me here to this earth even though her mom was mean
You see
I look at my dance
As I dance in the wind and breathe child yes I breathe
'Cause she lives on in me
With assistance from the clouds

I cook
Wear her shoes
Clean till I can't clean no more
But I now have all the things my mom wished for me
Yes, I am dancing
Yes, dancing
For all this is surreal as I kneel
And stop dancin' for a moment
I am sure that if I dance
When I dance
How I dance
Though I dance
Oh I dance
Through my dance
Although my dance
Is not in vain
In time
It will Rain

"First Person"

I
Because I
Because of I
I am a dream
I
Living as I
Breathing as I
I am the truth
I
Dealing as I
Stealing as I
Often do
And I
Want to be as I
Wanting as I
Want you
I
Loving as I
Holding onto
I
Are you the beginning?
Of I
Sometimes that I
Can't be as I
'Cause I
Am not to do

I
Don't care if I
Don't meet your expectations
See I
Wanna be as I
Wanna feel as I
Often do
I
Can't say that I
Wanna play as I
Need something real
With a real meaning
So I
Can grow as I
You know that I
Want to heal this feeling
I
I know that I
Won't act if I
Know everything
I
As Yours
As I
I do as I
Should wear your ring
I troubled as I
Can't tell if I
Will sink or swim
But I

I am
As I
Am in this game to win
I
Am your friend
Yes I
Won't lie to you
I
Even if I
Am not here
Yes I
Will send
You my love
That's time
I
You don't know that I
Search for an understanding
And I
Live on as I
With power in knowing
That with love
I
Am Everlasting

"Escapade"

And this
And this I thought
And this I thought would be real
And this
And this I thought
Would be forever
And this
and this moment
I had with you
I'll never forget
And this
And this
And this is the truth
And this
And this
And this I can tell
Is what I really want
What I really feel
And what
And what
And what
And what I can
Is only
But only
And only
Your lover
And this
And this

And with this
I am satisfied
For a time
And I
Cry when
You say you want more
But don't really mean it
And this
And this
And this I take for what it is
An Escapade
An escapade that will eventually end
That has its limits
And this
And this
And this is what I am
Happy for now
And this
I see that This Could change
Could change into something more
If you would open the door
If you could be my friend
If you could lend
Your hand to me
If you could hold
And protect me
Release me
Release me from you, Lover

Because
Whether you know it or not
I am in love
This love
Right now
Is mine
Mine in my heart
Mine in spirit
Mine in principality
And this
And this
And this love You take
And you know you take it too
But I am just your lover
And for some strange reason
You want me to be there
In the end
And this
And this
I tell you this
If I stop being
Your lover today
I'd see you cry too
It is because you don't want to leave
You want me
To be this
And be this
And be that

That temporary sensation
That moment of elation
That crazy connotation
That sexy flirtation
And that
And that
And that is not what I want to be
And I want
And I want
I want you to know how I really feel
And that
And that
And that which is the truth
Is this
I have you in my heart
Maybe we can finally start
To be more than an Escapade
More than just…getting laid
And just maybe
Just maybe
Just maybe I'd believe
You love me

"Wrong"

I can only do what I do
When I do what I wanna do
Wanna do what I do
Naw
You need ta
Do
What you do
And the only way you can do
What you do
Is if you do
What you wanna do
Just don't do
Nothin' wrong

"Blank as a Linen-Colored Rule"

When I think of all the torment
I suffered
Just because I was black
I shiver
When I feel I cannot make a sound
Because I talk too much
It will be a problem for me to keep it all in
And my face is blank
Just a stare
But I store my own words
Inside and I stare
My stare speaks for me
And sometimes I am perplexed
At how you
And you hate me so
It confuses me
That you want to be me
So I am blank as a linen-colored rule
And that is how I choose to be
You see
You can't read me
Or figure me out
Or understand my way
No one called you "The N-word" today
"What are they doing on our block?"
Is what they called out to me
And I just stared, my face blank in disbelief

*I am blank as a linen-colored rule
And I will never let you know me
I am strong and loud
Deep as the Black Sea
Don't try me
I choose to walk
With my head held high
And dare you to ask me why
I deserve to be all that I can
And maybe just maybe
You can see that I am what I am
Yes, I am blank as a linen-colored rule
And until someone
Decides to write my story
Only then will you
Know the truth
Because I only let you see
What I want you to see
And that
Is
Not me*

"Anyplace, Anywhere, Anytime"

Anyplace, Anywhere, Anytime
Only if I were yours and you were mine
You ask me to give myself to you
And I don't even know you
Any place if I know your face
For a while
You ask me to debase myself
And I don't even know your name
You ask me what I do
Where I go
So you can know
If you can take advantage of me
But you see
I am smart and I have goals
And nothing will deter me
From being in the know
So with all that you do
You better get tested
Any place, Anywhere, Anytime
Anywhere you go
And ask someone for sex
That you don't know
Can deliver the mark of death
Respect
You don't have for yourself
If you can ask me
And you don't even know me

If you can ask me
And you don't even know me
I dare you
To get to know me
I dare you
To like me even
I dare you
To tell me about you
And who your mother is
And where your father is
And I dare you to recognize
That there is something bigger than you
I dream
I dare to dream
And I will let no one turn my dream
Into a nightmare
So while you give away
Yourself to another
That you don't know
And who you are is on the low
You chance it
You chance your life and she
And time is wasted
So you better get tested
You see I haven't been tested in a year or two
But I for the past 10 years have said no to you
And everyone like you
Anyplace, Anywhere, Anytime
Only if I were yours and you were mine

"The lady in the wheelchair"

I could imagine it nice to have
Someone there when you need them
Someone to hold your hand
Someone to wipe the tears away
I could imagine it nice to have
Someone to hold you close
And catch you
Keep you from falling
There was a lady in a wheelchair today
Who had 3 people helping her
I wonder if I would ever have no one to
Help me if I were in need
And if I could even think of who would be there
They were patient and caring
And there was even a smile on her face
As she wheeled along
The 3 stood there chatting as they prepared
To transport her to her destination
As one held her pretty flowing blouse on
A hanger as I blew in the wind
I could imagine how nice to have
A caring smile
Someone to help you along if you need them
I should be able to find someone before it's too late
For me
Even though right now I'm not in need

And will it be too late
I once saw someone die alone
And I couldn't imagine being alone
When it's my time
So I make friends fast but they seem not to stay
They all seem to go their own ways
But I keep searching
I watched as the lady drove away
And imagined
Where she was going
And if there was another friend
Waiting on the other end to greet her

"I still do"

No matter where
No matter what
No matter who I may meet
I can't find anyone
Who could be
"the one"
I date
I skate
I take
I hate
I still do love you
No matter where you are
or wanna be
No matter what I may do
I can't find
Anyone like you
I cry
I lie
I spy
I tie
Myself up into two
I still do love you
No matter
No matter what you say
Now
Tomorrow
Today

"Master"

There is only one you
I could never find another if I searched
A million times
There is only one who can make me move
Make me smile
Make me scream
You
Control
Me
And I Love
You
Master

"This is not a Poetry Slam"

This is not a poetry slam
It is not whether I can speak words better than you
This is not a poetry slam
It is not that I know more or have gone through more than you
This is not a competition
A rise to the best
This is not a test
This is not a song that goes on and on and on and knows no end
This is not about me standing up here trying to make you my friend
No this is not about rhymes
'Cause poems you know don't have to
Don't have to sing
Don't have to scream
Don't have to talk
Don't have to walk across a page
They glide
This is not a poetry slam
A gain or defeat
A work or a skipped beat
For the transcendental elite
No this is not what people did in the sixties
When they couldn't eat
Not what we did to get across a message
I could sing it
I could scream it
I could whisper it
I could not say a word and look at you strange

And still hope after I leave from standing here off this stage
You remember my name
My name is Sha Rene'
You see
This is not a poetry slam
It is something I want you to read that one day I will write in a book
And yes it will take me some time
It will take me being disciplined
It will take me
Hopefully
To see you reading my words
Even after my life has ended
So this is not a poetry slam
It is
A feeling
A problem
A needing
A solvent
A truth
A message
A being
A delivery
A culture
That you don't see everyday
It is a
Trial
A tribulation
A message
For this nation

And I have said these words before
Probably in another poem
I repeat
A message of delivery that you don't see every day
Now I say it another way
This is not a poetry slam
It is existence for my words
That flow off the pages
And from my hands
To my pen
Or my computer keyboard
I give these words to you
This is a gift
This is my gratitude
My wealth
My health
My dignity
My tragedy
My grief
My strife
My strength
My weakness
My fight
You see with each word I want you to feel me
Not judge me
Not rate me against
Someone who wants you to feel them too

Each poem is individual
Each poem is the individual
Scratch that
Each poem is individual
Each poet is an individual
You see this is not a poetry slam
This is who I am

"And over there to the right on the bass"

He plays bass guitar
An' he don't give a shit
He does what ever he feels
And will give you back some lip
There's one thing I respect
Is that he don't care whatcha say
'Cause we all goin' outa this place one day
He holds his head up high
Though he doesn't have a dime
And sometimes
And just sometimes
He wish he were mine
But I can't let this feeling get over me
I am just waiting to see
When he goes back on Tour so I can
Cheer him on
That's what he lives for
His music and his son

"Ain't That Good News"

I used to cover my books in a brown paper bag and
I used to carry a metal lunch box with a handle
With the faces of the "Monroe's"
Funny how I loved that Western TV show
And I'd come home on afternoons
To watch the dogs down the block get sicked on me
It was hard living in Jersey City in the 60s
I watch Martin and John and Bobby get shot
And Ike, the reverend and the singer
Seemed so much alike alot
That I never knew the difference
I had a black doll and a white doll
And listened to Danny Kaye
Watched Mayberry and the Jackson 5
And wished all my troubles away
I got punched in the face for my lunch money
Ain't that funny
But I was abused as many girls were
And no one knew
A sin was to mention
A sin no intervention for me
So I sit in this place with wooden pews and
The good news is
I sit here in the dark

And the light shines
Through the windows
The windows are a stained glass with all these white people
On it that I don't know
And 'm 10 years old and I want to cover myself
In a brown paper bag
Just like my school books
And I look up at the ceiling

"Dis-Closure"

Mike
He stole my money
Said he wanted Christmas presents for his mother
or was it for his honey?
Jake
Lost his wedding ring in my toilet while
Trying to make himself feel more comfortable
I didn't now he was married till he lost the ring and freaked out
Tom's
girlfriend called and asked me why my number was in her man's pocket
Bobby's
girlfriend called and asked me why my number was in her man's pocket
Dan's
girlfriend called and asked me why my number was in her man's pocket
And he told me she was his maid
Tim wanted me to make love to his girlfriend
John
Insulted me by calling me his Nubian Queen
Don't he know he can't do that?
He's white
Steve
Wanted me to clean his house
Ted
Kept goin downtown to sell drugs
Donny
Called me from Folsom prison
Collect no less

Jerry
Invited me to his house to watch the fights
Lied and called to tell me he had a leak in his cellar
I knew it was a lie 'cause he called me the same night from his cellar
and I could hear a party in the back
Tim
Rode a bike to work instead of buying a car so he could get his kids some food
Jerome
Only saw me when his woman wasn't home
Hey I had never been to Harlem before
so I had no idea what would happen if she opened the door
And found me
Yeah but there was this one guy who I really liked
Tony
'Cause he wasn't no phony
He was real
Just he really wanted many girlfriends
To feel
Cedric left Gerry Curl on my couch
I wonder what that's was all about
Jim sells T-shirts on the beach
And still has that white girl's phone
And he wonders why I leave him alone
He is a nice guy though sweet and dear
he only works half the year
I need a man who works at least as much as I do

White Larry
Offered me Ten-thousand dollars to set me up in an apartment in NY
Let me tell you Larry
I ain't nobody's whore
Black Larry
Was cute but got into drugs but somehow he never forgot
That when I was outa college I enjoyed all his hugs
Then there was
Rick
My high-school beau
I loved him so
But he got into drugs too and a new woman to boot
So I left
Robert
I thought was my soul mate
We clicked on everything
And everything that's great
but he never left that women
Who came to my job to yell at me
I guess she had the right cause he wasn't free
After 3 years he finally left her
I was gone by then
To someone else
After 15 years we met again in the Bronx
I couldn't believe we kept thinkin' about our dream
That would never be
He had another woman by then you see
And drugs got to him too
Would you believe
And To His mom who loved me

Rest in peace

Will
was too old for me
Ed
was too old for me
Darren
Was too old for me
Tarik
I think was gay
He wanted to be that way
I can't go there
Michael
Tried to lock me in his mother's house
'Cause no one was home
I got outa there as fast as I could
Steven was too short
Hey I'm a big girrrl
Let's keep it real
Milton
was kinda scared
He was Spanish and had nice hair
Oh Well
Todd
Called a limo to take me to diner and a show
And cried 'cause I didn't commit on the first date
He was so low
Tim left me standing at the train
In the rain

Marcus
watches cartoons
Morning and noon
Morning and noon
Should I give him a spoon?
Kevin
left me on the side of the road in Newark to flag down
Someone to fix my dead battery
He said he didn't wanna get his hands dirty
Josh
Who was born again
Asked me to dance on his lap
Boy did I give him a real slap
Kaye
From Africa
asked me to help him sign his kids
To a famous Eddie Murphy movie
You knew the one
That was on the first date
I wasn't born yesterday
Demetrius
He is hot
But I can't really say
If his name should be in this poem or not
If your name is not in this poem, then don't worry you have no exposure
For those whose names are here
This is my Dis-Closure

"Statistic"

1 out of 4
1 out of 3
1 out of 2
This is what happens when you listen to someone other than you
1 out of 10
would be the number if you decided to just be friends
first
1 out of 3
1 out of 2
1 out of 1
is what happens when you want to just keep having fun
and you die you see we don't have to lie
no one has to paint you a pretty picture
There was a time we had to worry about the white man killing us off
now we kill off ourselves
I have been searching for my black man
And a black man has been searching for his black woman but finding someone else
Since the out house and the in house had its conflicts
Since the Man let you walk around in your pretty outfits
And get too beside yourself
All they had to do was watch you dance
And you been dancing in black face for a long time
1 out of 5 is a lie
That may be the number of slaves that managed to break free
I would be curious if those same black slaves who born a son who's son born a son
Is one out of 5
Like me

"To the Black Poet"

Are you ready to write a verse for me
To show me
Or tell me
Or Make me believe who you might be
Are you ready to write a verse for me
To sing to me
Breathe for me
Simply see that I could be interested in you
Are you ready to take me to the highest high
I never had b4
Are you ready to open the door
To say more
To give me love and send me pain
Even though right now
You don't know my name
Are you ready to write a verse for me
To challenge me in a bold step to reality
To make it all real
Are you ready to take my heart
From the start
And steal it
Let me know
'Cause I just wrote this verse for you
And I'm true to myself
And if you call
555-5555
You might find someone special in your life

Djembre

To the 808
And the TX81Z
And the R8
Who kept up the beat with me
To the
DMX
And the RX7
When the SP12 came out
We were in heaven
To all of you that put down beats
Here is the history
Now I'm goin way back
Way back to a
Djembre

To tha beat Ya'll

"Great Love"

You made me smile
You made me laugh and when I had something really important to
Talk about you would always listen
You are my idea of a man
That I always had in mind for me
I respect you
And always will
No matter what good times or bad times we may
Happen to see
I know you are still there
Even if in the background
There are no words to describe what I feel
When you walk into a room
No man has ever made me really feel
You know me
And allow me to be
When you call my name you make me weak
And make me seek for your beck and call
I met you at a bad time in my life
They say everyone in their lifetime
Has one Great Love
You are that for me

I am this is for you
That Great Love

"A Crossroads"

My Uncle
He is so talented
I hope to be as talented as he one day
He had an idea
An idea that
Blacks
Could Speak
Talk aloud
Mean to mean something more
To make those who don't know us
Maybe know us
This place
Old broken-down building
For Black actors
For the likes of people like Debby Allen
Or Phylicia Allen at the time
Or Eugene Lee
I will remember his eyes forever as he spoke aloud on a
STAGE
Act one, Scene one
My Uncle
Yes you had an idea
And someone tried to take it away
He at a Crossroads
Received a Tony Award
And I am proud
This poem is for Kenny

They call you Lee
And you
You are my mother's brother
I
Want to keep singing
I sing now through these words
Hey Uncle
I am working on a play
That
Maybe you can produce one day
Until then
I will keep on Crossing Roads
Over the waters
Like you

"A Black Woman's Song"

I am the man and the woman
I am the King and the Queen
I am the Prince and the Princess
Not living her dream
I am the lover and the creator
Of all that is life
I am the husband and the wife
I am the cook and the chef
I am the treasure and the chest
The peanut butter and the jelly
I am the salt and the pepper
The food in your belly
I am the maid and the butler
The book and the book maker
The idea and the dream
I am the sun and the moon
In the same scene
I am the mother and the big sister
The child and the parent
I am the son and the daughter
Isn't that apparent?
I am the court jester and the fair maiden
The spade and the diamond
The club and the heart

I am the rook and the bishop
Those are not so far apart
I am the guidance counselor and the teacher
The father and the mother
I can't breathe because I have worked so hard
I can't work any longer
I am the afro and the braid
And the long luxurious mane
I am the closet and know exactly what to wear
I am sexy as hell even when my stockings have a tear
Oh what the hell
Just rip them off
And as quiet as a mouse
But you mess up once
And you will certainly hear my mouth
I am walking up stairs and carrying stuff on the train
And crying 'cause I am tired
Of standing in the rain
I am the drops on the umbrella
That someone didn't hold over my head
To keep my dry
Today a man walked in front of me
to get to through the door to get inside
I wuz startled wondering why
I am the question and the answer

The truth and the lie
I am often alone
And on my own
Though folks are around when I die
I am the cleaner and the duster
The mop and the pail
And sometimes when I get a chance
I can go and get my nails done
I am the bookkeeper and the secretary
The boss and the worker
And this list is so long
It seems I can't go on any further
I am God because he made me
The servant to the one who should be my king
I am washing the dishes and not wearing a ring
I am the mediator and the attorney
Who sticks to the rules
And won't let anyone make a fool outa me
You see I am the one who never stops and works all day long
Like a dog
I am the Black Woman's song
I am the prayer and its blessing
I am the offering and the feast
I am the one who you think of the least
So I scream so I can be in your face
The club and the heart
And you will hear me aloud
I am the sky and also the clouds
I am the planets and the stars
And I always go farther than you

To a place that you can't find
No matter what you do
You will never know
Or try to understand
That I and only I am the woman who is born from the largest land
From where makeup comes from Khol and diamonds
In the mine
And my sugar is so sweet that
You leave them all behind
I come from cloth of rulers
And Egypt and the Nile
And now you see me in a vile light
Broken and shattered, torn all apart
Pouring out and delivering my heart
I am the ice that gets crushed
And the pick that's long
I am a Black Woman's song
Singing to God for help
To be my assistant
When I am supossed to be the assistant

Singing to Glory
As I fill the church with my lovely voice
I am the suggestion and the choice
God has chosen
Yes, God has chosen
Me

"Am I?"

King
Lord
Jesus
Brahman
Krishna
Jehovah
Elohim
Kaba
Shaddai
Olam
Yahweh
Allah
Dywok
Nebi
Shang Ti
Puruhuta
Allaha
I
Am

"The Ball"

A man once met a woman
and lucky was she to find someone so gentle and so sweet
A man once met a woman and said hello
A man once met a woman and she fell so deeply too fast
All she wants is for this love to last
and friends tell her to say goodbye but she can't
A man once met a woman
and lucky is he to find true love
and anyone can say they love you
anyone can be thinking of you
but are they willing to sacrifice themselves
or risk it all
or even give it all away if he ever wanted to go somewhere else
some day
A man once met a woman
and all she can do is think of how for once
she felt like Cinderella
for once she knew that even though it was raining on her glass slippers
she didn't need an umbrella
because she had this fella that would keep her warm and safe
A man once met a woman who has dreams and one of those dreams
was to be able to love someone to give to someone a great love
A man once met a woman and now he is guilty of causing her pain
and she still walks in the rain
and she cries herself to sleep if she can sleep
and she awaits for him to come to her and say he wants true love too
A man once met a woman who thought he walked on water
knows he has a daughter and a son and she would love them as her own

A man once met a woman and now she feels all alone again
and he wants to be friends
and in the end she is afraid it will not turn out like she wants
a fantasy that dreams are made of to be real
so she can feel
A man once met a woman who dared to step out and be free
be free and be with me
A man once met a woman who now doesn't know what to say and not sure
if she can get through each day now that she thinks he is gone
She took off the glass slippers because they were wet and now they are ruby I bet
because she now travels down the yellow brick road
hoping for a wizard
someone to look into a crystal ball and tell her what is next
a man once met a woman who wants to travel with him
on a journey and if friends first that is fine if this leads to a road
where cars are not left behind
and know that she likes fast cars that can go real far
but now she is putting the brakes on and not racing 'cause there was a bump in
the road
she still drives but a little slower now quite cautious but the engine roars still and
revs
and I am still in this race
I never give up
A man once met a woman who believes that there is love
and it is the only thing worth fighting for
She has opened the door that she feels God has planned.
So thank you for giving me a moment
a moment in time of complete happiness
A man once met a woman that dreamed of a man
and put it in her mind that it could be 4 ever

and wants Love that's all
Will she be going to the ball?
Dance with me

"Daylight"

I don't care where you live or what you make
As long as you correct all of your mistakes
I'm not broken or a fool
And I don't have too many rules
I am loving and kind and I sometimes think am I out of my mind to dream?
To dream that someone would hold my hand one day
To dream that every man I meet would not go away
To dream that he could be my friend
To dream that someone will be with me in the end
I don't care if you walk or run
As long as we can have fun and smile in the sun
But it's daylight
And I will know if this is right with you
You see
It's the things that you say and do
It's the opportunity you let pass by
It's me always wondering why
And maybe I think too much
But you see
You touched me
You touched my mind, my body and I am saving my soul
for one who deserves it
Could it be you?
I can control my mind and my mind can control my body
But dare to say

Dare to say to someone you care
Dare to live a dream
Dare to open your eyes to a life
That really means something and Dare to Love
I don't care if you don't have somewhere always to lay your head
If you lay with me in my bed for a moment
and dream
Then it's Daylight.

"White Butterfly"

Restless and awake at 4
and can't stop thinking of him
Restless and awake at 4
Wondering what he is doing
her friend
Restless and awake at 4 hoping he is happy
Even if not mine she has only best wishes for him
Selfless is he who loves so deeply he can let it go
never thinking but she hopes that one day he will be at her door
He needs to know that for not one day
has he ever left her dreams
and that he was the only one who was a perfect match for me
Restless and awake at 4 means
she gets her tea alone
Going back to everyday doing all things on her own
Restless and awake at 4
means she notices the difference
when so many men call her and just want sex
she gets very indifferent
so she walks quietly now and wonders if there was something she could
have done to get to sleep by 1

Restless and awake at 4 gives her a glimpse of tomorrow calls
and the weekend dates
and hates when they are not man enough to open the door for her
or pull out her chair
or whisper in her ear without putting their tongue in there

When they don't call her Darlin' or don't call her Hun
and don't wake up with the sun
and don't feed her soup or smile when she wakes
She can tell they are fake
When they don't hold her hand or they don't kiss her gently
They kiss so hard it hurts
or they don't move her in a way that makes her even want to put on a skirt
When they grope her so hard she pushes them away
and certainly she doesn't think of them every day

Restless and awake at 4
was what she was before she met her King
but he is not ready for that kind of thing so she waits
He said friends first and she didn't listen
I think it was the only time she remembers being selfish so she is sorry
Sorry for thinking she could make things happen sooner than planned
She wakes at night asking
How could he be the only man she ever met who ever fit?
She is not a quitter so will abide by his wish

Restless and awake at 4
For days and days she cried
Thinking he had lied
No
He was noble
He just walked away because the King wasn't ready for a Queen on that day
He has to be a Prince for as long as time permits
and oddly enough he had met a Princess who thought she was Queen
She wasn't ready for a King

*So now she sits at her Piano and sings
and goes on each day open to learning more*

*Restless and awake at 4
not knowing what is next.
She hasn't made up her bed
and misses his caress
No one had ever made her feel this way so she will just go on as he asked
and remember and be his friend and she hopes to see his face one day
and talk and laugh as long and hope one day they can wake at 1
and not be Restless anymore*

Like a White Butterfly I rise and it is morning now

Write

*I wanted to write
this
just for you*

Oscar Night

I thank from my heart always first in my life, God.
I thank my mother whose eyes always brightened when I told her I created something; a
song, a poem, a short story, a dress, a sketch, a painting, She was as excited as I was.
When my first 12" single, "I'm good for you," hit the radio in the late 80s my friends were so surprised.
I always do the things I say I will do.
I thank my best friend, Leslie Blau, for singing with me as a child.
I thank my enemies. Boy that's deep!
I thank my grammar school music teacher Barbara Brandeberry.
I thank the greatest of inspiration to me, Maya Angelou, who paved the way for all writers of freeform speech
and spoken word and the poet, yes the poetess.
I thank Damali Ayo for giving me the courage not to censor my sentiments.
I thank my New York photographer for 20 years worth of great head shots, Jim Kriegsmann Jr.
I thank all the Stages I have performed on.
And to the new Stages where my feet have not yet placed themselves. I will see you soon.
I thank my college buddy, Felecia Collins, for letting me sing behind her great guitar.
I thank theater creator and director, Kenneth Lee Richardson, my mother's brother, for letting me go into his Crossroads Theater as a teenager and listen to Black actors speak.
I thank Jerry Gant for letting me know what it feels like to stand in a bookstore like B&N and read my poetry.

We used to get together on Friday nights, and thanks to everyone who came to listen to my Spoken Words!

Sha

Sharon Rene Summers has been writing poetry since the age of 10 years old. Her first collection of poems entitled "Thoughts Come to Mind" is an eclectic collection of poetry with a variety of themes and topics written in her childhood using vivid imagery.

This new collection of works in the book, "Words Can Explain" was inspired from social experiences in the here and now capturing her inner emotions and feelings.

Sharon is a published singer/songwriter. She will be singing, playing music or performing her "Spoken words" at a café, club or stage near you. Look for her in your local bookstore. She is currently working on a play and wants to publish her lyrics of over 250 songs. Sharon resides in Southern New Jersey.

"I cannot find my roots standing because it is as if I have never fallen"

An excerpt from the poem "Roots" in this colorful poetry book of:

"Spoken Words"

by:

Sharon Rene Summers

Experience the words. They explain!

Printed in the United States
100694LV00003B/32/A